Life

Is a Nonstop Event

Life
Is a Nonstop Event

Carole D. Bos

Baker Books

A Division of Baker Book House Co
Grand Rapids, Michigan 49516

© 1996 by Carole D. Bos

Published by Baker Books
a division of Baker Book House Company
P.O. Box 6287, Grand Rapids, MI 49516-6287

Printed in the United States of America

Library of Congress Cataloging-in-Publication Data

Bos, Carole D., 1949–
    Life is a nonstop event / Carole D. Bos.
       p.   cm.
    ISBN: 0-8010-1104-3 (cloth)
    1. Women—Poetry. I. Title.
PS3552.07567L54 1996   96-43029
881′.54—dc20

To the memory of
my beloved grandmother

Alice Kooiker

Of the many good people
I have known
in my life,
she alone was a saint

Contents

9

Acknowledgments

*W*hen Richard Baker asked me to write a book of my reflections as a professional woman, my concern was finding the time. As a busy trial lawyer, I could not conceive of tackling the project now.

But something happened to me. Within a week after Rich's suggestion, I began to write. I could not control the flow of words that poured out of me. During the middle of the night, my husband would gently say, "Just get up and write what you're thinking about." I did and soon the project was completed. Rich, I am grateful for your suggestion; it gave me focus. Jim, I am thankful for your indulgence, help, and encouragement. That tolerance gave me freedom to write. Your criticism has been invaluable.

Sometimes university professors wonder if their message gets across to students who think they know more than they really know. Twenty years ago, Dr. Anthony Pariese told me, "You write about what matters but you do not take time to reflect. Stop rushing around so much and take the time you need to write well." Dr. Pariese, all these years I have remembered what you said. I have finally taken the time. Thank you for your honesty.

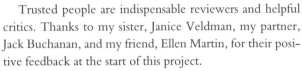

Acknowl-edgments

Trusted people are indispensable reviewers and helpful critics. Thanks to my sister, Janice Veldman, my partner, Jack Buchanan, and my friend, Ellen Martin, for their positive feedback at the start of this project.

I owe more than a debt of gratitude to my dear friend Susan Brent Millner. She helped me draw the pieces together; she gave me insight; she asked the tough questions that helped the words to flow. Susan, you are a sister to me.

I am grateful, most of all, to God who put the thoughts in my heart and the words in my mind.

Foreword

This book is about life—my life. It asks the questions I have asked myself. It considers the answers I have found. But in this life we never find all the answers, and there is no end to our questions.

The search to understand my life means I must be willing to look deep inside myself. I need to explore the emotional scope of my life. I need to consider why events happen when they do and as they do.

Sometimes answers are obvious; often they are obscure. Answers must lead, I think, to peace of mind, which for me is the ultimate objective. But in a world of turmoil, where life seems out of control and change constantly causes disorder, how does one find peace of mind?

My quest is to identify what we human beings can control and what we cannot. My resolve is to make peace with the things that "just happen" and to take charge of my response when they do.

Positive thinking alone is not sufficient to help us make our way through life; it only prods our initial motivation to live life to its fullest. Rather, inner strength that stems from faith and confidence sustains us as we travel ways

Foreword

that include false starts and wrong directions as well as smooth paths and super highways.

This book is, therefore, a celebration of the power of personal faith. I have found that my faith is the fuel that drives my life as well as the foundation on which I live. My poems reflect the truth of that for me. My hope is that they will also motivate the readers to discover the truth of that for themselves.

Journey

*L*ife is a wonderful journey.
The trip is filled with
Excitement and discouragement,
Laughter and pain,
Joy and sorrow.

Our control over life's events varies
From
No control
(When things just happen)

Journey

To
Total control
(When we act
Either constructively or destructively).

The human response to life's circumstances
Covers the spectrum of behavior
From
Extreme depression
To
Absolute joy.

I look at my life
As a nonstop event
Fueled
By the power of personal faith.

From faith I draw my strength
To live my life
To do my work.

My reflections here
Are mirrored by my soul.
They are my thoughts
They show how I look at my life
When times are good;
When times are bad.

Events of life
Are personal
But emotions and issues
Are universal.
Being human means
We all face difficulties;
How we respond is unique
To each of us.

My reflections
Raise questions
And explore issues
That have helped me examine my life:
Where I have been right
Where I have been wrong.
Where I have sought joy
Where I have felt pain.
Where I have faced danger and uncertainty
Where I have found safety and peace.

I hope
That my gift of thoughts
Will help your life's search
For understanding
For fulfillment
For contentment.

Losing Grandma

She had only a fourth-grade education;
But Grandma possessed more wisdom
Than anyone I have ever known.

She never went to medical school,
But her hands on a fevered brow felt better
Than any doctor's hands ever could.

She never went to seminary,
But her life was a clearer testament
Than any formal theology.

She always said she didn't know much,
But to me what she knew mattered most.

When I was young I loved to be with her,
Especially on Sundays.
When it was cold Grandma wore a coat
With a fur collar.
I liked to rest my head
On her shoulder
When I sat next to her
In church.
She and her fur collar were soft and comforting.

She made me feel
  Safe
  Warm
  Loved.
I thought that Grandma was a saint.

Losing Grandma

When Grandma was old and frail
She fooled every doctor who cared for her.
"She won't live through the night," they said.
But she lived nearly a year longer.
"Independence" is what she called her resolve.

"I never knew it would be this hard," she'd say;
But Grandma never let on how hard it really was.
"She doesn't understand how close to death she is."
    She did.
She planned her funeral.
"Keeps the details simple for everyone else."

People say,
"Well, she had a good, long life."
   She did.
Maybe that's why we miss her so much.

When she married, her pa had just died,
So her wedding dress was black.
She had a simple wish at the end:
To wear that eighty-year-old dress to her grave.
   She did.

"Ma, why do you want to wear
That old dress?"
"Ma, why don't you let me buy you
A new one?"

Her black dress had a collar
Of ivory lace.
The collar had not lasted those eighty years;
It was yellowed and frayed.
Grandma didn't mind.
"The collar can be replaced, can't it?"
  It was.

To Grandma,
The only dress worth wearing
At the end
Was the one she wore
At the beginning
Of her adult life.

She would have liked how she looked in it.

Why did she insist on wearing her wedding dress?
  I know.
She believed she was going to meet Grandpa;
She hadn't seen him in twenty-two years.

Grandma wanted to meet Grandpa
In death
As she had met him
In life:
Wearing the same dress she wore

At the start of their life together
On earth
At the start of their life together
In heaven.

I know what my grandma knew.

Models of Love

When I had no concept of sacrifice
I learned from two people
Who gave up much for their children
My father
My mother

When I had no idea about commitment
I observed two people
Who are dedicated to each other
And to their children
My father
My mother

When I had no understanding about honor
I heard the words of two people
Whose hearts are pure

My father
My mother

When I wasn't sure that truth is always best
I watched two people
Whose integrity is beyond question
My father
My mother

When I had no worries about financial security
I saw two people
Take extra jobs to provide for their family
My father
My mother

When I could not have cared less
About the meaning of life
Two people showed me the way
My father
My mother

When I first comprehended love
I recognized it because two people
Were loving to each other
And to their children
My father
My mother

*Models
of Love*

Today
When I muse on
Loving life models
I need look no further than two loving people
My father
My mother

Scars

*T*he wounds caused by cruelty
Of children to children
Create scars that last a lifetime.
I know. I still remember
Thirty-three years later.

How can a child exhibit
Utter innocence at one time
And calculate malice at another?

Where does the cruelty come from?
Is it inherent?
If so, can it be tempered?
Is it learned?
If so, can it be eliminated?

Scars

It's hard for children to endure
The wounds of humiliation.
It's hard for parents to help,
Since they frequently don't know.
Kids are too embarrassed to tell.
They often think they deserve what happened.
Thirty-three years have passed,
And I still haven't told my parents.

In junior high school I tried out for cheerleading;
I had been a cheerleader before.
For some reason—I never knew why—
The student body picked the cheerleaders that year.
For some reason—I never knew why—
The student body jeered me off the floor.
For some reason—I never knew why—
Some students asked, "Were you surprised by
    what happened?"
For some reason—I never knew why—
They laughed in my face as I choked back the tears.
For some reason—I never knew why—

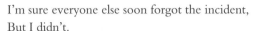
Scars

I was too humiliated to tell my family.
I guess I thought they'd eventually find out—
Everyone else knew.

I'm sure everyone else soon forgot the incident,
But I didn't.
I'm sure everyone else thought it had been
    a joke,
But I didn't.
I'm sure no one else remembers the story,
But I do.

I learned from the humiliation
To try never to humiliate anyone.
I learned from the hostility
To try never to hate anyone.
I learned from the public jeering
To try never to publicly embarrass anyone.

Maybe the incident helped to develop my character;
Maybe it's made me more sensitive;
Maybe I'm better off because it happened.

I didn't think so at the time.
What child could?

My Husband

When you gave me a husband
You gave me a best friend.
Thank you for that.

When you gave me a husband
You gave me a lover—
Someone to show me that tenderness
Can be a way of life.
Thank you for that.

When you gave me a husband
You gave me someone who
Balances me
Protects me
Helps me
Loves me.
Thank you for that.

In a world with too much hate
You have given me a safe harbor.
In a life with too much adversity
You have given me serenity.
In a land with too much violence
You have given me security.

It could have been different.
Marriages fail
Wives are battered
Children hate their parents
Lives are unfulfilled
When relationships lack
Love
Support
Honesty
Trust
You.

My Husband

Help me, Lord, to make my marriage strong,
Help me not to expect more than I should,
Help me to get it right
When so much around me is wrong.

Help me to be grateful to you
For giving me the foundation on which
I am building my life.

Happiness

*T*hree weeks after our wedding we moved to Europe.
We had not completed our college educations,
We didn't speak the language,
We didn't know the customs,
We didn't understand a whole lot about life on any continent.

Between us we earned less than $150 a month.
Our rent was $100.
We were a couple of kids
Embarking on a new adventure.
We struggled.
We were happy.

Many years later some things are different.
We completed our college educations,
We learned the European language,
We grew up.

33

Happiness

We know a bit more about life.
Together we earn more than we need
  each month.

But some things are the same.
We still struggle,
We are still happy.

It wasn't lack of wealth
That made us happy before.
It isn't possession of material things
That makes us happy now.

It's the intangible parts of life
That we embrace:
Best friends
Building a life together,
Fellow strugglers
Supporting one another,
Mutual achievers
Caring what happens to each other,
Pals
Playing together,

Lovers
Being together.

We are different sides
Of the same coin.

That's happiness.

Unborn

I couldn't carry my children to term.
I lost them before they were born.
  I never held them in my arms;
  I never taught them to speak;
  I never taught them to live.

  Why?

Is there a reason for the loss
  I have not known?
Is there a lesson in the loss
  I have not learned?
Is there a truth about the loss
  I have not seen?

  Is "Childless" who I am?

It's hard not to cry at a christening,
Not to get out of control
When someone asks the inevitable question,
How many children have you?

Do I have children?
Of course.
I count them
Although they were unborn,

Although they never looked into my eyes,
Although my daughter's little dress
Hangs in the closet unworn.

Will I ever find something to fill
    The emptiness in my heart?
Shall I look for something to replace
    My children I still long to love?
Will I ever get past my sadness over
    Losing what I wanted most?

37

Unborn

If there is a reason for the loss,
  I need to know it.
If there is a lesson in the loss,
  I need to learn it.
If there is a truth about the loss,
  I need to see it.

Help me, Lord, to find the meaning
  Of me.

Moving On

I watched my sister's anguish
When her daughter was stillborn.
I felt her pain even more
When I couldn't carry my own children to term.

I asked myself,
How do I get past the grief over loss
To focus on the joy over life that remains?

It is easy to become captive to grief,
Tempting to dwell on what was taken.

But if I did that—
If I allowed myself to stay distracted—
I would give the best of my time to the one who is gone
At expense to those who most need my love:
Children who are alive and require my attention,
Family members who also have suffered a loss.

Moving On

I have had to move on
Notwithstanding emotional trauma;
I have had to move on
Notwithstanding permanent aches in my heart.

I can't eliminate the difficulties of life;
I can only manage their effects on me.
I can't eliminate the ache in my heart;
I can only stop the ache from taking over.
I can't eliminate the loss of loved ones;
I can only give my love to those who are still here.

Breaking Ice

*M*y husband said, "You ought to be a lawyer."
To this day he doesn't know why he thought that,
  But he was right.

At first I couldn't imagine such a thing.
  What do lawyers do?
  How do they do it?
  Are women lawyers?

I investigated the field.
  It appeared to be interesting.
  Few lawyers were women;
  I thought I could be one.

But how would I become a lawyer?
  I knew no lawyers,
  I had no connections,
  I lacked inner direction.

Breaking Ice

I went to work in a firm
To see if I understood law,
To see if I could handle its intricacies,
To see if I liked lawyers.

Attorneys in the firm tried to discourage me:
  You can't work full time and attend school.
  Women shouldn't be lawyers.
  Women surely can't be trial lawyers.

I decided to be a trial lawyer.
I thought it would be good to break some ice.

After graduation I wanted to work in the same firm.
  The partners voted no.
  I was out.
  Why?
  Was it me personally?
  Was it my gender?

No one said I didn't work hard.
No one said my work wasn't excellent.
No one said, "You can't handle the load."
No one denied I was the only young lawyer in the firm
Whose writing had made *Law Review*.

Yet the ice I had broken left me in a huge hole.

Breaking Ice

"It's in your best interests to go elsewhere."
I never understood why my view of "best interests"
And theirs were not the same.

I had to leave the firm.
But where would I go?

One lawyer believed in me.
We left the firm together.

Breaking ice has interesting results.
  I had to find solid ground
  And stand on my own.

At first I wanted the lawyers who had rejected me
  To see they had made a mistake.
  I wanted to be better,
  To work harder,
  To be more skillful
  Than they had ever imagined.
  I wanted to show them
  A woman could succeed in the legal profession.

I proved my choice had been no mistake.
  I did my best,
  I worked hard,
  I used all my skills

And showed myself I could be
A successful woman,
A successful lawyer.

I learned
To focus not on the hurdles
But on ways to get over them,
To align myself with positive thinkers
Not with naysayers,
To swallow pride
When it's hardest to do so,
To explore alternatives
When I don't want to think about change,
To recognize that some of the best results in life
Stem from the worst of circumstances.

Now that I stand on solid ground
I can mentor other young women.
I tell them
Success is not about male versus female—
Thinking about that is a complete distraction.
Success is never quick and easy—
It only results from hard work and constant struggle.
Success is not about self-praise—
Let others say your work is good.

I also tell them
   Success is rewarding—
   Use those rewards to help others.
   Success is satisfying—
   But never be satisfied only with past results.
   Success is addictive—
   So learn to control its effects on your character.

Yes, I broke some ice,
And now I stand on solid ground
Where my continuing effectiveness lies
In my success
At melting ice.

Avoiding "Pollyanna"

"Pollyanna" and I used to be inseparable.
We were soulmates—
Our thinking was alike
   On most difficult issues:

   "We can handle it."
   "Of course I forgive you."
   "What else can I do for you?"
   "Make the best of it."
   "Life is beautiful."
   "I trust you."
   "Let's share the credit."

Then early in my career,
Pollyanna let me down.

Avoiding Polly-anna"

I worked with people
  Who took advantage of good intentions,
  Who ridiculed innocence,
  Whose words and deeds were hurtful:

"You handle it."
"Why should I forgive you?"
"What else can you do for me?"
"Why should I care?"
"Life is what's best for me."
"You can't trust anyone."
"I'll take the credit."

I started to avoid Pollyanna;
I thought I needed
  A tougher
  Stronger soulmate.

Worry became my companion:
   Would I become too cynical?
   Would I develop a negative attitude?
   Would I risk nurturing
   A martyr syndrome? A "poor me" attitude?
   Would being "tough enough" hurt my marriage?

Avoiding "Polly-anna"

I don't avoid Pollyanna anymore.
Now I selectively share her attitude
   When it's appropriate.
   We're not inseparable;
   I still trust innocence and good intentions.

I don't know any other way
To keep my professional world
   FROM
Interfering with my personal life.

I've decided:
I'd rather have Pollyanna
   Let me down
   THAN
Live inside a tough shell
   Where my guard is always up.

The Dark Side

All my life I'd heard about people
Who use others for their own gain.
All my life I was warned about people
Who have mastered the craft of deception.
All my life I knew about people
Who will blatantly lie to get what they want.

Never in my life did I believe I would be
A victim of greedy maneuvering;
Never in my life did I think I would mistake
A manipulator for a friend.

I was wrong.

I should have known better.
"This will either work well or
Our friendship will be over."

Why would friendship be over
Unless it were misused in the first place?

I ignored the warning signs.

All my life I'd heard that people
Have a dark side.
All my life I was warned that
Negative emotions can be dangerous.

Never in my life did I anticipate
How strongly I would wish ill toward someone.
Never in my life did I suspect
How intensely negative my thoughts could be.

What happens when trust is destroyed?
   The impact of broken trust
   Whirls the core of emotion
   Into unknown territory—the dark side of character.

What is it like to face the dark side of character?

I never thought I had a dark side
   Until I was betrayed;
Then I discovered extraordinary hostility.

The Dark Side

I never thought I could completely cut
  Someone from my life
  Until I was used;
Then I discovered unbelievable anger.

I never thought I could discard
  Someone I believed was a friend
  Until my friendship was abused;
Then I discovered hatred.

I never thought I could ignore
  Someone who needed me
  Until I realized the need was a lie;
Then I discovered profound bitterness.

Hostility, anger, hatred, bitterness
Are part of the dark side of my character.

When I first realized this

  I didn't like what I saw,

  I didn't like what I felt,

  I didn't like who I was.

I didn't know how to control the negative emotions.
I wasn't sure I wanted to.

For a time
  Anger clouded my thinking
  Bitterness impaired my judgment
  Hostility monopolized my attitude.
Seeing the dark side of my character
Made me afraid of the hatred that possessed me.

I became determined
  Never to be manipulated again,
  Never to be vulnerable again,
  Never to succumb to selfish lies again.
Still, I could not purge
The terrible thoughts from my conscience.

I felt like I was standing in wet concrete
That was quickly hardening
Me
My response
My character.

If I did not leap out of the concrete
My perspective would be controlled by anger,
My attitude would be managed by fear,
My regrets would last forever.

Wearily I faced the dark emotions of my soul;
I resisted the power of their hold on me.

53

The Dark Side

I struggled to walk away from
The temptation to seek revenge.

The dark side still has some control
    Over forgiveness,
    Over forgetfulness.

Love does not return easily when anguish is deep;
Prayer does not come freely when greed
Has sliced at the core of a relationship;
Trust is not quickly restored when
Trustworthiness has been doubted.

Only when I recognized the grip
That negative thinking had over me
Could I fear its hold enough to know
I had to let go.

But I could not let it go
    Without prayer,
    Without reflection,
    Without time
To think about the consequences of my actions.

I have learned that
    Good persons are capable of evil thoughts,
    Positive thinkers are subject to negative emotions.

I am grateful that
I am more resilient than I had thought,
 Especially when I seek direction,
 Especially when I look to God for help.

Responsibility

*W*hen I was a girl
It wasn't my job to take care of things;
My parents took care of me.

When I was a teen
It wasn't my worry to provide for things;
All I had to do was help.

When I was a young woman
It wasn't my concern to watch out for others;
I had all I could do to watch out for myself.

Now that I am an adult those things are
My job
My worry
My concern
My responsibility.

If I make a mistake
It's my own fault;
If I get off the track
I have lacked focus;
If I unintentionally hurt someone
I have been inattentive;

Respon-
sibility

If I misspeak
I haven't properly prepared;
If I lose my way
I have failed to ask for help.

Nearly always the failure is mine
Even though sometimes it's hard to admit.

Admitting fault
Is part of taking responsibility;
Accepting responsibility
Is part of life.
It's a hard part of life.

Facing up to a mistake
Can be a miserable experience;
I have learned that blaming others
Makes me more miserable in the long run.

Whenever I admit the failure
I am free to change course.
Whenever I acknowledge the wrong
I am free to make things right.
Whenever I accept responsibility
I am free to grow as a person.

But
When I don't admit the failure was mine
I am stuck in the old course.
If I don't acknowledge the wrong
I am unable to set things right.
If I don't accept responsibility
I am incapable of becoming the best person I can be.

So I give myself the freedom
To make the responsible choice
Of taking the responsibility
In which I will find freedom.

*Respon-
sibility*

On Failure

*P*eople say,
"Life is what you make it."

If that were true
I'd have made my life free of
Debt
Worry
Fear
Anxiety
Despair.

People say,
"Life is what's handed to you."

If that were true
I'd have capitalized on
Intuition

Talent
Motivation
Ambition
Drive.

My friend says,
"Life is beyond anyone's control."

If that were true
I'd have seen no point in
Thinking
Learning
Working
Striving
Changing.

I have failed,
I have succeeded,
I have been afraid of failure,
Which drives me to succeed.

Failure does not occur in a vacuum;
Neither does success.
They are intertwined in the process of life,

On Failure

For the human goal
Is to outweigh the
Failures by the successes.
"Failure" doesn't always mean
Down
Nor does "success" always mean
Up.
For without down
There is no up,
Without setbacks
No victories ahead.

"High achiever"—
Blessing and bane.

My life has taken strange turns
Unexpected highs
Have led to
Unanticipated lows
Absolute losses
Have turned into
Wins
Sure wins
Have become losses.

A loss was not ultimate failure;
Nor a win true success.

On Failure

Some of my greatest accomplishments
Have followed monumental failures—
But only after
I have learned the lessons from failure
I needed to know for success.

Brush with Death

*B*efore I could do anything
A semi demolished my car.

I heard the first crash.
The sound reverberates in my head
When I have close calls even now.
I thought I was going to die then.

Spinning out of control,
Gas leaking everywhere,
I felt the second impact.
A utility pole stopped the spin;
It almost stopped my life.

I was stunned when I heard the officer say
It was my fault.

What stop sign?
What ticket?
To this day
I don't remember seeing the sign.
How could I have missed it?

I was shocked when I realized
How little control I have over my life.
One second I was fine,
The next just short of dead.

I marvel over my having been spared.

Circumstances were not in my favor.
The first impact was squarely on the gas tank,
The second against the utility pole.

One inch farther
And I, not the car only,
Would have been wrapped around the pole.

The recollections make me shudder.
They also make me grateful.

The police officer said I was lucky:
The seat belt saved my life.
I say I was blessed:
God saved my life.

This I know:
Whether I lived or died
Was beyond my control.

Getting Sick, Being Well

$\mathcal{T}$he doctor's words were abrupt and unexpected:
"We'll start chemotherapy right away."

Chemotherapy? for what?
I feel just fine;
I'm not that sick;
You must be wrong.

What does it mean?
I'll lose my hair;
I'll lose my looks;
I'll lose my life.

It can't be true.
I'm still too young,

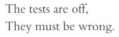

*Getting
Sick,
Being
Well*

The tests are off,
They must be wrong.

The doctor's words were abrupt and unexpected:
  "It's getting worse."

It must be true.
I don't feel well,
I don't look good.
It's such a waste.
Why does life end so soon?

My body is ill
But my soul is strong.
I need to fight;
I won't give in.

And then, with time,
I make my peace.
I grasp what once
Seemed out of reach.

I'm calm
About my lot,
About my life,
About my soul.

The doctor's words were abrupt and unexpected:
  "I think you're well."

How can this be?
I had no chance;
I was so ill;
I had no choice.

As I look back, the pieces fit somehow:
Growth follows pain;
Calm follows fear;
Hope follows shock.

Now I have peace of mind.

As life goes on,
This memory cannot fade.
It will sustain
When crisis strikes again.
I've faced the worst;
I've been refined.

I'll be equipped
Next time.

Balancing Acts

I live an interesting life.

My life has one problem:
  I haven't learned how to balance it.

Whenever I try "to do it all,"
  I know I'm doing little very well.

When I spend too much time working,
  I know I'm delinquent at home.

When I take care of things at home,
  I know I'm ignoring obligations at work.

When I spend time with my friends,
  I know I'm slighting my family.

When I spend time with my colleagues,
  I know I'm not tending to the needy.

The cycle goes around again.

If I spend more time at work,
   I feel guilty about not staying home.

If I stay home,
   I regret the pile of paperwork in the office.

If I take an afternoon to read a good book,
   I fret until I clean up the kitchen.

If I take a week off,
   I wonder how I will be prepared to do my job.

I used to try to handle everything,
   But that didn't work;

I was doing more
   And accomplishing less.

To no one's surprise but mine
   I got sick.

I decided I had to cut back,
   But that didn't work.

I worried more about my "undones"
   Than I credited my "dones."

Balancing Acts

Now I have settled on doing my best
  With my time, my obligations, my energy.

My life still is not in perfect balance.
  But I am fairly comfortable
  With my state of relative imbalance.

I live an interesting life.

Renewal

When the rigors of work overwhelm me,
   When the day-to-day strain is too much;
I need a safe place I can go to,
   I need a safe harbor for rest.

I never thought much of respites,
   I was above needing them
Until I got sick, then I worried
   My life would be over too soon.

Now I take time when I need it—
   Though sometimes it isn't enough—
To rest for a day or for a whole week.
There are times when I need to escape.

Renewal

I've found the safe harbor I turn to
    When work overwhelms my life.
It's an island that's blessed with such beauty
    Only God could have made it that way.

The house stands on top of a mountain,
    The view leaves me speechless each time.
The beach nearby is the best in the world;
    To me this is God's paradise.

Each evening the sky is a sketchbook
    Of stars that I think I can touch.
When I stand at the window and stare up above
    I'm amazed I've been given so much.

I was changed at the end of the first week;
    The island's now part of my life.
It pulls me back whenever I'm worn;
    I cannot resist its strong tug.

On this island of much matchless beauty
    I can rest without cares or concerns.
Within a short time my strength is renewed;
    I'm ready to go back to work.

Yet I know the next time I'm tired,
    Overwhelmed with the day-to-day strain,
I will go to the mountain where the view is superb.
    The island is beckoning me.

But when I can't get to the island,
   In the greater part of the year,
I still need to carve out a piece of each day
   For renewal, reflection, and rest.

On normal days it's a struggle
   To find ten minutes to think
About what I must do and where I must go;
   Life is a nonstop event.

But I need to resist the temptation
   To let outside influence control;
My life is my own to direct and to guide;
   Inner strength will move me ahead.

Renewal

If I don't permit time to ponder
　About life and the people I love,
I won't have the strength that I need for each day,
　I won't have the wisdom to lead.

I have felt the strength of renewal,
　I know its incredible force;
The need is to make time where it doesn't exist,
　To develop learned habits of choice.

The Partners

I needed some help with the workload.
   I was traveling and working too much,
I had little time for the housework,
   Domestic things weren't getting done.

I told my husband I needed
   His help. "You have to do more."
But husbands pretend that they don't know
   How to do things inside the home.

"That's women's work"—the first comeback;
   "I can't" follows closely behind.
It's always the same, it's part of the game
   That lets them do nothing at all.

"You need to do more, hon, I mean it."
   He meant well—he always does.

"Tell me what and I'll do it."
  My response: "Can't you see it yourself?"

It isn't my way to nag him,
  It isn't my way to sulk,
It isn't my way to grumble,
  My way is to do it myself.

But after a while I was finished
  With doing the housework alone.
After all, I was working and helping
  With his side of our marriage vows.

So I thought that I'd show him directly
  About cleaning and washing and chores.
I decided to stop doing laundry
  No matter how dirty things got.

There were mounds of clothes in the laundry,
  The underwear soon was all worn;
No clean clothes were ever forthcoming
  Except mine, which I did for myself.

I never said one word about it,
  I never told him my plan.
I was cheerful and loving and not once did ask
  Why his clothes were in piles on the floor.

After he did his own laundry
   Without asking how it all works
We talked about what had transpired
   And my transparent, life-changing trick.

We talked about how it's not easy
   To do all the jobs we should do;
We talked about how it's not fair for the wife
   To be sole caretaker at home.

But I also learned a big lesson.
   I'd thought that I shouldn't care
About fixing the car or the roof or the shed
   Or the eaves or the screens or lawn chair.

If snow needed shoveling, he'd do it,
   If grass needed mowing—the same;
Mechanical things made me shudder to think
   Of the knowledge I lacked about them.

I learned we have different perspectives
   That can gnaw and lead to conflicts.
But if we sit down and talk it all through
   We need not resort to the tricks.

The Touch

*U*ltrasound revealed the diagnosis,
  The fetus had almost no chance.
Doctors posed the question,
  Should the child be carried to term?

"Almost no chance" signaled hope,
  Hope that the child could survive.
The mother's heart made the choice:
  To fight against all odds to win.

The child was born with a defect;
  Without multiple surgeries he'd die.
The surgeon was blessed with the knowledge
  That could help the small child pull through.

But what is the skill of the surgeon,
   And what is the role of machines,
If the mother's choice to go forward
   Conflicts with the odds to survive?

What more than the surgeon's sure knowledge
   And more than technology's power
And more than amazing medicine's strength
   Can save the life of a child?

Help from the prayers of the mother,
   A boost from the strength of her will,
And the living hope she holds in her heart
   For the life she holds in her arms.

The Touch

A family's faith in God's love,
　　And the power of his healing hand,
And his blessed touch on the child—
　　Each was a part of his plan.

The surgeries were finally over,
　　The baby's defect was healed;
A child who'd had almost no chance at all
　　Is now normal and healthy—alive!

No matter how people regard it,
　　No matter what thoughts they express,
There's one reason alone for the outcome—
　　The child was saved by God's touch.

Teaching Teens

It's hard to teach someone who knows everything.
  Teens know they know best—so they boast.
It's hard to tell someone who's not yet eighteen
  That he's making a terrible mistake.

It's not easy being a teenager;
  It's not easy living with one.
My friends had a son with talent and charm
  Who possessed a strong will of his own.

His choices in general were wise,
  But like everyone's, some had been dumb;
He made a bad choice, his folks said, "Change,"
  But he followed his buddies instead.

The battle raged on, but the teen didn't budge;
  He left his parents no choice.

"Either you change or you pack your bag."
    He thought they were bluffing, of course.

When he realized they were not bluffing,
    His bags had been packed and locks changed.
He came home to find a note on the door:
    "We're sorry, you're not welcome here."

He knocked on the door but couldn't get in,
    For the first time he knew how things were.
He went to his friend—where else could he go?
    But that welcome didn't last very long.

He got through to his dad: "Why can't I come home?"
    "You can, but you know what it takes."
But still he didn't want to live by the rules;
    Still his key couldn't open the door.

Before long his life on the outside
    Led him to think, "It's a drag."
But the issue of pride—of admitting a wrong—
    Kept reconciliation at bay.

Time mellows most things—even pride of a teen.
    When reality shook him he knew
That his parents had had his best interests at heart,
    And that he had disrupted their home.

Maybe his life on the outside
    Caused him to see and agree
His rebellious disruption had been out of line,
    And his only recourse was to change.

Now things were different; he couldn't just show up
    And merely say, "Hi, here I am."
Now he must ask to be taken back in;
    His old home was no longer his.

Returned he was also repentant,
    But no one was sure that would last.
Yet to his credit he had transformed his life,
    And his parents had met him halfway.

As I watched all of this, I wondered,
    Could I have asked him to leave?
Would I have listened to all of his pleas,
    Given in to his passionate talk?

My friends said they'd utilized "tough love."
    But exactly what does that mean?
From my view many aspects of life
    Can be tough and solutions unseen.

Whenever I think of my own life
    I remember the ups and the downs.
Love can be tough even when things are fine,
    And it takes a strong will to stand ground.

Teaching
Teens

Years now have passed since the lockout;
    The recalcitrant teen is a man.
As I watch him today I'm convinced that he thinks
    He may use the same method someday.

When I think back I ask the hard questions:
    What if he'd never come home?
What if he'd said, "Your rules stink . . .
    Have a nice life—I'm on my own."

What if the ending weren't happy?
    What if he'd never conformed?
What if he'd never learned and returned?
    What would the family be now?

If he'd rejected his folks and his home,
    Would his mother and father have thought
That the method hadn't been worth the results?
    Would they wish they had sooner pulled back?

As I sit back and ponder these issues,
    It is clear there is no easy way
To teach teens about the tough side of life
    Nor to determine tomorrow today.

Nicole

*B*aby Nicole was born beautiful.

Baby Nicole had spina bifida;
She would never walk independently;
She had water on her brain;
But no one knew
What she could do.

As Nicole grew
She learned to walk with crutches;
A shunt diverted water from her head
To her stomach where it did no harm.

Nicole had expressive eyes
That sparkled when she smiled.
She did not know that she was different;
Her birth defects were normal to her.

Nicole

But even Nicole's normal life was at risk;
She could not live without her shunt.
If it became disconnected and remained unrepaired
Her brain would be irreversibly damaged.

When things go wrong
Small children cannot report;
Crying isn't eloquent enough
To say what hurts.

When Nicole's shunt became disconnected
No one knew
What the consequences would be;
No one knew
How fast the pressure would build inside her head;
No one knew
How or where the enormous amount of water would exit;
No one knew
It would find a way out through her brain stem;
No one knew
She would have massive brain stem herniation;
No one knew
How close to death she would come.

When I first met Nicole
Her eyes did not sparkle;
She could no longer see.

Her crutches were in the closet;
She could no longer walk.
Her childish prattle had ceased;
She could no longer speak.
I tried to help her family
Put the fragments of their life back together.

Life's fragments are sometimes all we get.
Nicole's mother asked me,
"Why my daughter?"
I had no answer.

Nicole is now twelve.
She still cannot see
She still cannot walk
She still cannot care for herself.

But Nicole has life.
She has some ability to speak.
She has enormous ability to bring joy
To her family
To her friends
Every day.

Future life for Nicole is uncertain;
She is at risk for infections, complications.
Her mother worries.

Nicole

Who will care for Nicole
When she no longer can?

But Nicole is happy.
She attends school,
Even though her ability to learn
Is extremely limited;
She knows the bus route by heart,
Even though she cannot see it;
She knows the names of her friends,
Even though she can scarcely converse with them.
She loves music;
It helps her to be calm.

Nicole's mother has learned
To be calm.
She no longer asks
"Why my daughter?"
She now understands
Nicole's life is meaningful,
Nicole's life has purpose,
Nicole's life is special.

Just like Nicole.

Never Was

I saw my friends' marriage disintegrate.

They both seemed powerless to stop
   The arguing
   The alienation
   The anguish.

There was a time when it seemed they could
   Communicate
   Listen
   Understand
   Love.

I never understood what went wrong.
   Maybe I'd misread the match,
   Maybe the match never was right
   And they had only wished it so.

But if it was never right,
  How would they know?
  How would they change?
  How would they salvage?

How do they tell their children
  It was a mistake?
  It was doomed to fail?
  There is no turning back?

Can there still be healing for
  Hurtful accusations?
  Insensitive remarks?
  Unkind scheming?
  Greedy manipulation?

Will they ever get over
  The pain of separation?
  The trauma of betrayal?
  The sting of loneliness?

If there are no winners, only losers,
  Can the loss ever stop?
  Can the pain ever end?
  Can the wounds ever heal?

And should I, a friend to both,
  Take sides?
  Intercede?
  Interfere?
  Keep silent?
  No.

I, a friend to both,
Can try to
  Be available unconditionally
  Give advice sparingly
  Provide support immeasurably
  Understand indefinitely
  Care abundantly
  Be a true friend.
  Always.

A Visit from an Angel

*W*hen the baby was born
He looked like an angel—
Everybody said so.

As the toddler grew
He was a perfect child—
Everybody thought so.

His grandpa
Became the child's closest friend—
"Papa Jim" he called him.

The child
Became his grandpa's greatest joy—
"My pal" he called him.

Life for the grandpa
Had never been so rich,
Had never been so meaningful,
Had never been so happy.

Christmas would be special.
The two-and-one-half-year-old was excited—
Presents under Grandpa's tree were for him.
His innocent chatter filled Grandpa's heart
With fascination.

Then, suddenly:
Virus incurable,
Convulsions uncontrollable,
Respirator disconnectable.
Oh, God!

In his little white coffin
The child looked like an angel—
Everybody said so.

During his short life
The special child had touched hearts—
Everybody thought so.

A Visit from an Angel

The child's love
Had warmed his grandpa's heart
As it had never been warmed before,
Had lit up his grandpa's life
As it would not be lit again.

Yet,
The old man was left with the sense
That he had been in the presence
Of an angel.

Special child or angel;
Christmas Child eternal;
Old man hopeful.

Guardian Angels

I visited the Holocaust Museum
At the same time my close friends
Were in Washington, D.C.
I had not known of their plans;
If I had, I would have warned them that
The exhibits would be too difficult
For their young children.

As I passed through the narrow aisles
People bumped into me at every step.
The architect had intended it.
My friends were unaware
Of that intent.

As I passed through the narrow aisles
I was shaken.

Guardian Angels

Pictures of unspeakable horror
Shoes that had once belonged to the living
Suitcases carried by unsuspecting people
A cattle car that had carried families to their deaths
Surrounded me
Surrounded my friends.

The experience was heartrending for me;
It overwhelmed my friends.

Family members had perished in the Holocaust
Exhibits brought the horror home
The children were crying
It was hard for them to breathe.

The children had to leave quickly
But how?
A stranger tapped my friend's shoulder.
"You are thinking of leaving
But do not know the way?"
She had not said that to anyone;
She had only thought about leaving.

Stunned, she accepted the stranger's help.
He guided the family out so they did not pass by
Pictures of skeletons
Photographs of dead villagers

Rail tracks from Treblinka
Artifacts from daily life
Stolen then discarded
Elements of close family life
Destroyed by intruders.

The stranger led them out of the museum
Using a way they would not have found
On their own.

Arriving on the street
My friends turned to thank the stranger,
But he was gone.
They never saw him again.

My friends are convinced the stranger
Was an angel
Sent to protect them.

I think they are right.

We talked about it.
  Do guardian angels really exist?
  Where do they come from?
  How do they get here?
  How do they know
  Who needs help?

Guardian Angels

The literal answers didn't seem to matter
At the time;
A guardian angel had led that family from
The darkness of emotional turmoil to
The light of day.

Today I wonder:
    Why had angels not helped
    When many had cried
    Before?
    Where were the angels
    Over there
    Back then?

Easing Loneliness

The old woman in the nursing home was frail.
She looked like everybody's grandma.

She was alone, yet she always seemed preoccupied
With thoughts of years past,
With hope for days to come.

No one came to see the old woman.
It didn't seem to matter to anyone—
Not even to her.

Her present life was focused on the past and the future.
She spent her days reminiscing about times long ago,
She spent her nights thinking about life after death.
The present was irrelevant except
As a tool for her reflections.

*Easing
Loneliness*

She seemed
Lonely
Lost
Lifeless.

As I watched her, I wondered,
Will I end up this way?
What happens when time slows down?
How many hours can we think the same thoughts?
How many days can we revive the same dreams?
How many months can we recreate the same life?
How many years can we be alone?

I spoke to the old woman.
"How are you?"
Surprised to have a visitor, she smiled.
"Oh, I'm alright.
Is it Christmas yet?
When will the children be here
To sing the carols?"

Easing Loneliness

How might I tell her
Summer winds still blew,
Christmastime was still far off, and
Months would pass before the children came to sing?
Time stands still for those who are alone.

For me, watching someone who is truly alone
Has been a great teacher
Of life lived
Of kindness needed
Of love required.

Fear of being alone myself
Helps me to understand the loneliness of others.
And if I understand, I can ease
The loneliness of those for whom
The present is but a bridge
Between what used to be
And what is yet to come.

Success

*M*y friend asked me a question
I could not readily answer.

"Why do people who lie and cheat
Always seem to do better in life
Than people who try to do the right thing?"

A philosophical answer would not do;
She needed a practical response.

A theological answer would not do;
She already knew what that was.

We examined a specific case that troubled her.
An employee was told to fake product test results,
If he lied, people might be harmed.

Success

He could not lie so he was fired.
Someone else faked the results;
The product was made.
The company is successful;
The former employee is bitter and destitute.

Her question to me:
"Why was evil rewarded and good punished?"

She wasn't satisfied with the standard answer:
"The case isn't over yet;
We don't know the final outcome."

It wasn't the final outcome she cared about.
"Why did doing the right thing
Produce such bad results?"
And more importantly,
"Why does that always seem to be the case?"

I couldn't give her a quick response,
But her questions made me wonder.

Is apparent success true success?
Is it incorrect for me to think
That outer and inner successes could be different?
Is it true that the pain of doing right

Ultimately prevails over the ease of doing wrong?
How long will it take for the fired employee to believe
That what he did was in the end best for him?
What if he never believes it was best?

I too have heard the quick, standard answers:
Doing the right thing is always right.
Without suffering you can't experience true joy.
Striving is the essence of life.
You can only gain after you experience pain.
Everything always works out in the end.

Yes, I know that getting to the end matters,
But how I get there matters most.

I have learned
The quick, standard answers are true
But they don't ease the day-to-day struggle.
They don't give me all the help I need to live my life,
For living life is no simple matter.

I'm just beginning to understand the adage
"Wisdom comes with age."
A successful life
Always incorporates good and evil,
And in the struggle
Sometimes evil seems to prevail.

Success

But while I'm in the midst of the struggle
I cannot say that evil has won.
Only when I have crossed the bridge to the other side
Of the conflict can I call the results.
Only after I have experienced the entire event
Can I say which side has won.

That takes time—
Sometimes a lifetime.

The Concept of Faith

I met a man whose philosophy of life
Didn't seem to offer much:
> At sixty-two, my high-level executive days are over.
> After thirty-seven years, my wife and I are unhappy.
> My children are failures.
> I think I am too.
> When it's time, I'm going to end it like Hemingway.

What made me happy, he wondered.
> My faith.
> My marriage.
> My family.
> My career.

He scoffed at the concept of faith:
> I came from crap;
> I'm going back to crap.
> If I die like Hemingway, at least I decide when.

He laughed when I said
    I didn't come from crap;
    I'm not going back to crap.
    There's no reason to blow off your head like
        Hemingway.

His response was that
    The only point of life
    Is just to live it
    Before we disappear into oblivion.

I asked him about
    The point of living—
    If just living life
    Merely gets us to oblivion.

He said
    It doesn't matter.
    He was satisfied with his lack of faith
    In anything but the here and now.

I argued that
    It does matter.
    Faith in nothing but the here and now
    Is no faith.

He pondered my question:
    If you really have faith in nothing,
    Which has brought you only sorrow,

How is your lack of faith better than my faith,
Which has brought me only joy?

Intrigued, he smiled but said nothing.
We became friends, though.
Maybe that was his answer.

I still wonder
Why he told me about his inner turmoil,
Why he told me about his pain,
Why he told me about his despair.
Did he think it would bring a measure of peace?
Did he think it would ease his pain?
Did he think I could somehow help lessen his despair?

I know
Another person's understanding does offer some peace,
Kindness does ease pain,
Candid talk does help lessen despair
When someone openly questions
The meaning of existence.

Maybe my friend saw in me
  The power of personal faith.
  Maybe that recognition made him question
  The strength of his doubt.

I often wonder
  Whether our talks mattered as much to him
  As they mattered to me.

Time

I saw a bouquet of dried roses today.
That made me think about time.
I realized the roses didn't bloom very long.
That made me think about life.

I thought about how I look at my life
And how I think about time.
I've adopted a mindless lack of respect.
I don't care unless I'm far behind.

I wondered if the fragrance was strong
As the sun helped the buds come of age.
When the petals were fresh, did anyone see?
What if no one smelled them till now?

Time

By the time I know what my life is about
Too many roses will die.
Other flowers will bloom once I'm gone.
How much will I miss until then?

It's true that fresh roses are here a short time.
It's true that my life is the same.
I struggle to find the essence of life
But distractions prevent many gains.

All of these years of mismanaged hours
As I studied time management books,
I frantically searched for what isn't there.
I have usually misunderstood.

I've thought about time as something to sell—
A commodity—not a true gift
I can give to me, to my family and friends.
But I've lost more than I ever sold!

After I saw the dried roses today
I thought about time's forward thrust
Its mechanical ticking of minutes and hours
Its swift, ineluctable span.

With its unceasing movement and unyielding force
Inexorably rushing ahead
Time holds my life, but I let the clock stop.
I think about what I have left.

Time is a gift, not something to sell.
It's mine to control as I choose.
I'm going forward now with strengthened resolve
And respect for what once I abused.

Beyond Youth

I'm 45 now.

My hair is turning gray
Like my grandma's
Like I didn't want it to
Like I knew it would.

My laugh lines are becoming wrinkles
Permanently, I guess
Inevitably, I guess
Acceptably, I guess.

My body isn't the same
I can't run as fast
I can't do as much
I can't go as far
As before.

What does it mean to age gracefully?
Is that a euphemism for getting old
Wishing for what once was
Longing for what never can be?

Beyond Youth

I wouldn't be normal not to think that
I want the body I once had
I want more endurance
I want to turn heads again.

Sometimes it's hard to celebrate the
Appreciations:
With age comes understanding
With maturity comes wisdom
With long life comes respect.

More often it's easier to denigrate the
Depreciations:
Pretty young women on the beach savor admiration
While mature women want to avoid embarrassment
Pretty young women are daring with their clothes
While mature women look for ways to cover up.

Help me, Lord, to know that
Flat stomachs can't replace firm resolve
Strong thighs can't replace solid insights
Outward good looks can't replace internal beauty.

Help me to believe that
Gray in my hair won't dull my zest for life
Lines on my face won't diminish my inner glow
Extra weight of my body won't slow me down.

Help me, Lord, to be
Content with who I am
Happy with the life I have
Satisfied with where I am today
Grateful for what I had yesterday
Hopeful for where I will be tomorrow.

Beyond Youth

Journey's End

During this journey
I have displayed the road map of my life.
The map is filled with
Rough roads and smooth,
Straight roads and winding,
Busy roads and quiet,
New roads and old,
Closed roads and open.

Your life's road map may be similar;
Likely it's different.

On your life's journey
You, like me,
Find yourself on roads
You have not intended to take;

How you travel those roads
Is a choice you make.

On your life's journey
You, like me,
Find yourself on the very roads
You intended to take.
How you travel those roads
Is a choice you make.

Journey's End

On your life's journey
You, like me,
Face roadblocks, detours,
Must change direction.
How you determine your direction
May or may not be
Your choice to make.

But

At the end of the trip
Know that
You have coped with events
Beyond your control,
You have achieved
Peace of mind,
You have found your way,
You can applaud the journey's end.